The Little Princess & The Bubble

Written by her Daddy
Robert Bean

Illustrated by her Grandmother
Kay Bean

Visit our Website for more Little Princess and ordering!

http://www.littleprincessbubble.com

No part of this publication may be reproduced in whole or in part, or stored in a retrieval system, or transmitted in any form or by any means, electronic, mechanical, photocopying, recording, or otherwise, without written permission of the publisher
Little Princess Bubble Publications

Text copyright © 2010 by Robert Bean.
Illustrations copyright © 2010 by Kathleen Bean.
All rights reserved.
Printed in the U.S.A.

The author and illustrator would like to thank Kay's dear friends Sierra and Norman Rose for the initial layout and Scott Harrison for the final layout.

ISBN 978-0-615-36912-9

A Bathtime Story for Abigail

Once there was a Little Princess having a bubble bath. She saw a very big bubble. She leaned closer and put her finger to it. But it didn't pop the bubble. It just went straight in.

It was very bright and shiny inside the bubble.

Kay Bean

The bubble sailed over the lane where some children were playing.

They shouted and waved and ran along beneath the Little Princess in her bubble.

She shouted and waved back and laughed as the bubble floated up into the sky, over the trees at the end of the lane, and across the village to the beach.

But then the wind changed
and the bubble sailed
down,
    down,
        down,
over the sand.

It slowly drifted over the sea
and gently landed on the water.

The Little Princess rocked happily
inside her bubble on the deep blue water
with the sun shining through.

A kind fisherman in a small boat
saw her and came over to help.
As soon as he touched the bubble, it
∴ popped ∵
and the Little Princess fell
∴ splash ∵
into the freezing cold water.

She gasped and sputtered
until the fisherman gently lifted her into his boat.

"You look just like the Little Princess," he said.

"I am the Little Princess!" she cried, "And I'm very
upset about losing my bubble!"

The kind fisherman rowed the Little Princess to shore. Shivering, the Little Princess had to walk past all of the people on the beach until the fisherman's wife wrapped her in a warm blanket. Then the fisherman and his wife carried the Little Princess back home to the castle.

The Queen and all her maids rushed out to hug and kiss their Little Princess.

The grateful Queen rewarded the fisherman and his wife with a pouch full of gold coins.

Then, salty but cozy in her favorite nightie, the Little Princess told her mother all about her exciting adventure, while the maid served hot chocolate and cookies and prepared another hot bath.

www.ingramcontent.com/pod-product-compliance
Lightning Source LLC
Chambersburg PA
CBHW040032050426
42453CB00002B/98